Total Abandon

A DRAMA

by Larry Atlas

SAMUEL FRENCH, INC.
45 WEST 25TH STREET   NEW YORK 10010
7623 SUNSET BOULEVARD   HOLLYWOOD 90046
LONDON   *TORONTO*

Copyright © 1981, 1984 by Larry Atlas

ALL RIGHTS RESERVED

CAUTION: Professionals and amateurs are hereby warned that TOTAL ABANDON is subject to a royalty. It is fully protected under the copyright laws of the United States of America, the British Commonwealth, including Canada, and all other countries of the Copyright Union. All rights, including professional, amateur, motion picture, recitation, lecturing, public reading, radio broadcasting, television, and the rights of translation into foreign languages are strictly reserved. In its present form the play is dedicated to the reading public only.

The amateur live stage performance rights to TOTAL ABANDON are controlled exclusively by Samuel French, Inc., and royalty arrangements and licenses must be secured well in advance of presentation. PLEASE NOTE that amateur royalty fees are set upon application in accordance with your producing circumstances. When applying for a royalty quotation and license please give us the number of performances intended, dates of production, your seating capacity and admission fee. Royalties are payable one week before the opening performance of the play to Samuel French, Inc., at 45 W. 25th Street, New York, NY 10010; or at 7623 Sunset Blvd., Hollywood, CA 90046, or to Samuel French (Canada), Ltd., 80 Richmond Street East, Toronto, Ontario, Canada M5C 1P1.

Royalty of the required amount must be paid whether the play is presented for charity or gain and whether or not admission is charged.

Stock royalty quoted on application to Samuel French, Inc.

For all other rights than those stipulated above, apply to William Morris Agency, Inc., 1350 Avenue of the Americas, New York, NY 10019.

Particular emphasis is laid on the question of amateur or professional readings, permission and terms for which must be secured in writing from Samuel French, Inc.

Copying from this book in whole or in part is strictly forbidden by law, and the right of performance is not transferable.

Whenever the play is produced the following notice must appear on all programs, printing and advertising for the play: "Produced by special arrangement with Samuel French, Inc."

Due authorship credit must be given on all programs, printing and advertising for the play.

ISBN 0 573 64038 6   Printed in U.S.A.

No one shall commit or authorize any act or omission by which the copyright of, or the right to copyright, this play may be impaired.

No one shall make any changes in this play for the purpose of production.

Publication of this play does not imply availability for performance. Both amateurs and professionals considering a production are *strongly* advised in their own interests to apply to Samuel French, Inc., for written permission before starting rehearsals, advertising, or booking a theatre.

No part of this book may be reproduced, stored in a retrieval system, or transmitted in any form, by any means, now known or yet to be invented, including mechanical, electronic, photocopying, recording, videotaping, or otherwise, without the prior written permission of the publisher.

IMPORTANT ADVERTISING & BILLING REQUIREMENT

ALL producers of TOTAL ABANDON must give credit to LARRY ATLAS as the author of the play in all programs distributed in connection with performances of the play, and in all instances in which the title of the play appears for advertising, publicizing or otherwise exploiting the play and/or production, including playbills, houseboards, throwaways, circulars, announcements, and whenever and wherever the title of the play appears.

The name of LARRY ATLAS shall be in size, type and prominence at least fifty percent (50%) of the size of the type used for the title, and must appear immediately following the title of the play on a separate line upon which no other matter appears.

THE BOOTH THEATRE

A Shubert Organization Theatre

Gerald Schoenfeld, *Chairman*   Bernard B. Jacobs, *President*

ELIZABETH I. McCANN   NELLE NUGENT   RAY LARSEN
WILLIAM J. MELOCHE   PATRICK S. BRIGHAM   JOHN ROACH

present

RICHARD DREYFUSS

in

TOTAL ABANDON

A New Play by

LARRY ATLAS

with

JOHN HEARD   CLIFTON JAMES
GEORGE N. MARTIN

Setting by   Costumes by   Lighting by
DAVID JENKINS   **JULIE WEISS**   **BEVERLY EMMONS**

Associate Producers
MARC E. PLATT   SANDER JACOBS   TOMMY DeMAIO

Directed by

JACK HOFSISS

The Producers and Theatre Management are Members
of The League of New York Theatres and Producers, Inc.

CAST

(*in order of speaking*)

Lenny Keller	RICHARD DREYFUSS
Henry Hirsch	JOHN HEARD
Walter Bellmon	GEORGE N. MARTIN
Ben Hammerstein	CLIFTON JAMES

Place: A midwestern courthouse. The present.

THERE WILL BE ONE FIFTEEN-MINUTE INTERMISSION

STANDBYS
Standbys never substitute for listed players unless a specific anouncement for the appearance is made at the time of the performance.

For Lenny Keller—Jon Polito; for Walter Bellmon and Ben Hammerstein—Thomas A. Carlin.

TOTAL ABANDON was developed by Elizabeth I. McCann, Nelle Nugent and Ray Larsen at the Perry Street Theatres as a work-in-progress, directed by Jack Hofsiss, and designed by David Jenkins, Julie Weiss, and Beverly Emmons. The Perry Street Theatre production was funded by Walt Disney Productions. We gratefully acknowledge their support.

THE CHARACTERS

Lenny Keller is a workingman in his early thirties.
Ben Hammerstein is Keller's court-appointed attorney.
Walter Bellmon is the County Coroner.
Henry Hirsch is the court-appointed Psychiatric Examiner. By profession, background, and temperment, he is an outsider.

Total Abandon is set in the present in a city of one or two hundred thousand in the middle of America. The main playing area is a holding/waiting room in a county courthouse; it contains a table and a couple of chairs. The entrance to this "mainstage" is a single door upstage. At times one or more characters appear on separate, smaller sidestage(s) to the left and/or right.

Total Abandon

ACT ONE

At opening LENNY is alone on the main stage while HIRSCH and BELLMON converse on the side. The scenes should flow into one another with particular attention to the contrast in tone and rhythm.

LENNY. I always wonder why they call it "necking." Don't you wonder where that word came from?

HENRY. Doctor Bellmon . . .

WALTER. Yes, Doctor Hirsch?

HENRY. Dr. Bellmon, you know perfectly well that I was already a medical doctor before I began my study of psychiatry. I am fully capable of understanding the nature of these injuries.

WALTER. Of course, but I am talking about the causes.

HENRY. That is my specialty.

LENNY. I don't wonder why they call it "sparking." That's the one that makes sense to me, sparks flying and all. But how about . . . spooning? Where's that from? Lie down like . . . spoons? I mean . . . fit together, like that? My feeling is that that's a very lovely explanation for the use of that word.

WALTER. I mean the immediate causes, Henry . . . I mean, from an examiner's point of view.

HENRY. Yes?

WALTER. I mean how the injuries were sustained. Whether the victim was pushed or thrown to the floor, or against other objects; whether any weapons were used. If not, the type of blows struck by the assailant — slaps, punches, kicks, knees, elbows; the degree of force involved, the duration of the attack. All of this bears on the question of intent.

HENRY. Not in my opinion, Walter.

WALTER. You can't be serious.

LENNY. Those are words that my parents might have used. People my age most commonly used the phrase "make out," but I don't see that at all in the same vein. I was never able to bring myself to say that to a . . . to a . . . sweetheart of mine: "Would you like to go for a ride in my car, and perhaps we could make out."

HENRY. There's nothing in the recent literature to support a connection between motive and means, except in the most obvious sense.

WALTER. Which is?

HENRY. Only that the use of extreme force equates with the intent to do bodily harm.

WALTER. And that's as far as you will go?

HENRY. Yes.

LENNY. Well, I could go on at some length about the words and vocabulary of romance and love-making.

WALTER. So you would admit no distinction between an assault in which a weapon was acquired twenty-four hours in advance of a crime, and one in which the weapon was immediately at hand and employed in the heat of the moment.

LENNY. Perhaps a discussion of romance is not appropriate.

HENRY. No.

WALTER. Nor between an attack that took place over a period of hours or days, and one that occurred in a few moments of rage?

HENRY. Walter, the house of premeditation built on physical evidence has crumbled.

WALTER. I'm glad to see the house of humor has not.

HENRY. We can distinguish state of mind in many ways, but the points you raise are not among them.

LENNY. I knew this girl who writes music. And I tried to write some words for her. I really couldn't do it, but I did come up with a phrase I like, which is . . . "Though the tracks may disappear, the train rumbles on." I like that all right. I like words that say how things . . . vanish in the distance.

HENRY. There is a whole spectrum of tests and interview techniques . . .

WALTER. . . . evaluated within an entirely subjective framework, of course.

HENRY. Certainly. But don't you think the decision of the court will be largely subjective in this instance?

WALTER. Not at all. It ought to be decided on the merits, and on questions of law.

HENRY. But if the plaintiff is in earnest . . .

WALTER. Oh, come now.

HENRY. . . . the court will first want to determine whether the action springs from a genuine concern on the part of the plaintiff, or . . .

WALTER. Yes?

HENRY. (*brief pause*) . . . has some other motive.

WALTER. (*ironic*) I can't imagine what that might be.

(*They exit. Having entered a beat earlier, BEN speaks, without pause:*)

BEN. Let me make my position clear to you, Mr. Keller. You should know where I stand.

LENNY. Could you call me Lenny?

BEN. I don't think we should do that, Mr. Keller. For purely professional reasons.

LENNY. Well, then could you just call me Keller. That's kind of more familiar to me.

BEN. All right. As I was saying, I want to explain to you the nature of this hearing, the reason it's being held, and the immediate implication of the judge's decision, whichever way it goes.

LENNY. O.K.

BEN. First of all, you understand that none of what I'm discussing with you now has anything to do with how Tom came to be in the hospital, nor will that question enter into the ruling of the court in this matter.

LENNY. I understand that.

BEN. That's a completely independent issue, to be considered at a later date.

LENNY. You've made that very clear now, Mr. Hammerstein. I appreciate it.

BEN. On the other hand, there will of course be a description of Tom's medical condition, and there will almost certainly be some general discussion about what would cause such a condition. But I remind you there will be no . . .

LENNY. No what, sir?

BEN. . . . no attempt, today, to fix responsibility.

LENNY. Fine.

BEN. Then I'll review what the court *will be* considering.

LENNY. Mr. Hammerstein, may I interrupt you for a second?

BEN. Go ahead.

LENNY. You're not very happy to be involved with this, are you, sir?

BEN. Keller, you're . . . you're not stupid . . .

LENNY. Thank you, sir.

BEN. . . . and I'm sure you can appreciate that I have

personal feelings about my cases and the people I represent. But you can believe me that for as long as I am instructed to act as your attorney, I will do so without allowing those feelings to interfere. You can be confident of that.

LENNY. Well, I am, but I just want you to know that I'm serious about this . . . I'm not trying to . . . get out of anything.

BEN. Whatever, Keller. It doesn't matter. May I go on?

LENNY. It could be a lot of people might think I'm doing something wrong. I went to the hospital . . . the day after it happened . . . I went. I saw him there. I'd do anything to get him out of there, if I thought I could.

BEN. I . . . accept that.

LENNY. I tried to reach his mother. You don't know this, Mr. Hammerstein, but that was a very difficult thing for me to do.

BEN. I'm sure it was.

LENNY. I even tried to find her through . . . the last man she was with, that I knew. I didn't want to talk to him, you can be sure of that.

BEN. Mister . , .

LENNY. Please don't call me that. You'll never guess how I knew where she was, or rather, as it turned out, where she'd been. I got the address off a card she'd sent to Tom. It was on the wall by his bed. It said, "I am for you. Will you be my Valentine?" You know how they do: "I . . . M . . . 4 . . . U. . . ?" Big, lacey heart on it. 'Course this guy didn't know where she was, said she'd . . . travelled on . . . flown. It's pretty funny, actually, 'cause the second he picked up the phone I forgot the speech I worked out. Word one, I couldn't think of word one.

(*From the sidestage WALTER speaks as if delivering a report:*)

WALTER. At admission the patient's condition was as follows:

LENNY. (*as in a phone conversation*) It's Tommy . . .

WALTER. As revealed by superficial visual examination . . .

LENNY. No, I can't tell you anything about that.

WALTER. . . . multiple lacerations and contusions along the entire length of the right side of the body, and about the head, neck, and shoulders.

LENNY. The ambulance people were real good. They were working on him right on the spot.

WALTER. Apparent dislocation of the right hip. Apparent dislocation of the right elbow and right shoulder.

LENNY. (*forgetting the phone . . .*) I couldn't get anybody to tell me anything.

WALTER. Apparent fracture of the right femur. Obvious fracture of the nose. Apparent bi-lateral fracture and/or dislocation of the jaw.

LENNY. I just stood there. I couldn't see anything to do. I turned right around, went back home to get him some things. I didn't know what he'd need.

WALTER. Radiological examination verified complex fractures of the femur and the jaw, and further revealed hairline fractures of three ribs, and compression-type fractures of the second and third lumbar vertebrae.

LENNY. I do know that people like to have their own things.

WALTER. Completing this portion of the examination, a skull series revealed a multiform fracture of the skull in the area of the left occipit.

LENNY. I put his toilet articles in a bag. I got his pajamas. I didn't know if that was allowed. He has this cap he wears. I brought that. I wanted there to be something he'd recognize.

WALTER. A swelling of the abdomen and the presence of blood in the urine and vomitus prompted a surgical exploration which verified severe internal hemorrhage resulting from laceration of the liver; contusion of the lung, mesentery, and small intestine; and rupture of the spleen.

LENNY. He wears it tilted over on his head.

WALTER. Subdural hemorrhage was verified.

LENNY. I can only tell myself he doesn't have any pain.

WALTER. At the time of his admission the patient was unable to breathe without mechanical assist.

LENNY. . . . no pain.

BEN. Now, Mr. Keller.

LENNY. Please, sir.

BEN. . . . with regard to your son . . .

LENNY. Please.

BEN. . . . your son . . .

LENNY. Could you please call me Lenny?

BEN. All right. Lenny.

LENNY. Yes.

BEN. Shall I go on?

LENNY. I appreciate it.

BEN. Fine. Now . . . Lenny . . . your son has been declared dead by a panel of physicians appointed by the court for the purpose of making such a determination in accordance with the laws of this state.

LENNY. But I don't . . .

BEN. I know, let me finish. This same law provides for a one-time appeal of such a judgment. You have chosen to exercise that right of appeal. That is the purpose of today's hearing.

LENNY. Right.

BEN. Now the state will argue on behalf of the medical panel. I want you to know beforehand the kind of argument they will advance. I want you to understand what our response will be. And I want you to understand what the judge will take into account when he makes his decision. All right?

LENNY. Sure.

BEN. Among the purposes of this law, and the reasons behind its formulation are, first, to provide a definition of what constitutes a legal death in this state; and, second, to set forth a guideline for the cessation of extraordinary life-support measures when that definition has been fulfilled. Are you with me so far?

LENNY. Yes.

BEN. Now, the doctors who treated your son decided that, according to the criteria stated in the law, he was legally dead. In this state that means that he can't breathe and that his heart won't beat for any substantial period of time without medical aid; or that there's no spontaneous brain function.

LENNY. I understand that.

BEN. Fine. The doctors, acting under the law, went to the judge and informed him of their findings, and asked him to take the next step and appoint an independent panel of specialists to affirm their findings, which he did. As you know, this second group of doctors agreed with the group from the hospital that your son was dead. Under normal circumstances the next step would be for the hospital people to remove your son from the life-support . . . and that would be the end.

LENNY. Except that I stopped it there.

BEN. Indeed. What the judge has done, as you requested, and as the law provides, is to issue a temporary restraining order preventing the hospital from turning off that equipment. Now, the purpose of today's hearing is to decide whether the judge will issue a permanent injunction to keep that equipment on, or whether he will lift his temporary order and allow them to remove it.

LENNY. I can't . . . I can't see that.

BEN. I remind you that every doctor who has examined your son agrees . . . believes . . . that he is already dead.

LENNY. Sure, but I . . . believe . . . they could all be wrong.

BEN. Well, that will be the point I'll argue before the judge. But I think you should know there's a good chance he will find for the state, and lift that order. You shouldn't be overly optimistic.

LENNY. No, I wouldn't want to be that.

BEN. The law was written to settle disputes of this kind . . . well, not exactly this kind, but . . . you know what I mean. In this instance the legislature was remarkably precise. Unusually so. It seems to me your son's case falls rather neatly within the limits of the law's definition.

LENNY. Neatly?

BEN. Just don't expect too much.

LENNY. I have never had a problem in that direction, Mr. Hammerstein. You've made yourself clear.

BEN. Have I? In that case will you allow me to withdraw this appeal; put an end to the suspicions it will cause, the problems that it may mean for you later on?

LENNY. Mr. Hammerstein, you haven't by any chance been to the hospital to see my son?

BEN. There hasn't been . . . no, I haven't.

LENNY. Well, if you'd go . . .

BEN. Mr. Keller, another attorney can be assigned to act in your behalf. Would you like to have that done?

LENNY. Please, sir, I wasn't trying to say . . .

BEN. You can make *that* request. Would you like to?

LENNY. No, sir, I'm sorry.

BEN. *Will* you reconsider this appeal? (*LENNY shakes his head.*) All right. All right, then . . . as I said before, the cause of Tom's injuries is not relevant to these proceedings. I expect no . . . trouble . . . on that score. I will argue that although Tom's condition appears to fall within the parameters of the law, diagnoses of legal brain death have been in error in the past, and may again be so in this case.

LENNY. Do we have to go all the way into this?

BEN. (*containing himself, but insistent*) Yes . . . Lenny . . . yes. I will argue that there is no need for the court to rush to a decision in this matter.

LENNY. Please . . .

BEN. I will argue that if, as the state contends, your son is already dead, there can be no further damage to his dignity.

LENNY. Please, sir . . .

BEN. I will argue that dignity is a quality of the living, and that the maintenance of temperature and pulse and respiration in your son's body . . .

LENNY. Please . . .

BEN. . . . . is intrinsically no less dignified than the electrically produced twitch in the thigh muscle of a frog on a laboratory table. Will that . . . satisfy you . . . Lenny?

LENNY. Yes.

BEN. Fine. Of course, the state will argue the opposite. They will say that your son, living or dead, demands of us dignified treatment. You understand?

LENNY. Yes.

BEN. They will say that his body, living or dead, should be afforded a degree of respect, and that to maintain it in these circumstances is less than . . . civilized. I expect they will be very . . . forceful.

LENNY. It's only for the boy.

BEN. They will also try to cast doubt on your motives for bringing this action.

LENNY. I thought you said that wouldn't come into it.

BEN. Only in the form of a general suggestion that you are unwilling to face . . . the end of the situation. They can, and no doubt will, question you about this.

LENNY. About the . . . end of the situation?

BEN. Yes. The court may want to call for expert testimony on these matters; doctors, for example. They may want to question you beforehand.

LENNY. They've been here once already. They said they'd be back.

BEN. Were you cooperative?

LENNY. Yes. They're doctors.

BEN. Yes. Good. I think we've gone over all the material I wanted to cover. I'll go across the way and see where we stand now. I'll be back when they're ready for us.

LENNY. All right. Thank you. (*A pause as BEN starts out.*) Mr. Hammerstein?

BEN. Yes.

LENNY. If you . . . if you could get to the hospital . . . you could see how . . .

BEN. Keller?

LENNY. Yes, sir.

BEN. I don't mean to be abrupt.

LENNY. No, sir.

BEN. I'm leaving now. (*He exits.*)

LENNY. Leaving now? Well, I don't mean to be abrupt either, sir, but I believe I'll just be staying here, abruptly or otherwise. Hah! Abrupt. Now what the

Jesus is the obstacle to climbing into your Lincoln Mark forty-odd or your Cadillac Heat-wood, and going over to see the boy? There's that energy crisis gone and affected us again. No? Well, I didn't think it proper . . . or polite . . . to ask whether you had a boy, or how you felt abour your boy, or whether you'd go to visit your boy. If you did, or if you would go to visit mine, you wouldn't go on trying so hard to be so lofty. Regardless of the . . . situation. My son, I admit, isn't looking very well right now, but he doesn't look dead, and he doesn't look like some dead animal on a laboratory table. He looks to me like . . . like . . . I was going to say he looks like me. Wouldn't that be something? You can imagine how I felt when I went back there, my arms full of . . . belongings. Everything he's got has an animal on it. He's got a toothbrush, and the end is a little plastic rabbit. He's got a face cloth with birds, and he's got a bottle of shampoo in the shape of a teddy. He's got pajamas with ponies and coyotes on it. And he's got this cap with the face of an elephant on it. And he's got tubes coming out of his nose and his mouth, and he's got a tube going into his arm. He's got tubes in his belly. He's got a tube going into his little penis and he's got a tube in his ass. That's what he looks like. I say to myself . . . Jesus . . . this thing here is my seed. So I just stand there holding on to this A&P shopping bag full of his little creatures. Don't ever ask a question in a situation like that. You look too human. "Excuse me, nurse, could you tell me who's in charge?"

(*WALTER speaks from the sidestage as if opening his statement to the court:*)

WALTER. We must face the fact that technological advances in medicine . . .

LENNY. I had obviously popped the big one.

WALTER. . . . have generally outpaced the ability of the judicial system . . .

LENNY. I'm the boy's father. Could you help me?

WALTER. . . . to deal comprehensively with them in a manner consistent with . . .

LENNY. This one right here, he's mine.

WALTER. . . . the fulfillment of social policy objectives.

LENNY. Doctor? Doctor, I'm the boy's father. Could you tell me what his condition is?

WALTER. The plain fact is that medical technology . . .

LENNY. If you could just give me an idea.

WALTER. . . . capable of maintaining individuals indefinitely in a state of irreversible coma . . .

LENNY. Yes?

WALTER. . . . has blurred the definition of death . . .

LENNY. Well, I can see he's not in very good shape, but if you could say what's wrong with him . . .

WALTER. . . . and raised questions quite without parallel in the annals of medico-legal jurisprudence.

LENNY. Eventually, I set down my bag so that I could tell them I wasn't leaving the room until I got some answers. They don't like that.

(*His voice replacing WALTER's, HENRY speaks from the rear of the mainstage:*)

HENRY. Lenny?

LENNY. Sometimes I don't like the way certain people abuse their authority. I mentioned that where my son was concerned, I was the *only* authority.

HENRY. Lenny?

LENNY. I had a right to all the news, whether that

news was good or bad, and they had no right to withhold anything from me.

(*WALTER resumes in an explanatory tone, still from the side:*)

WALTER. Sir . . .

LENNY. You can bet that got some action. They don't like having the law laid down to *them*. It kinda loosened up some of the jaw-jackers in that very professional group. They told me — thank you, doctor —

HENRY. Lenny?

LENNY. . . . that my son had broken a couple of . . .

LENNY & WALTER. (*unison*) . . . ribs . . .

LENNY. . . . and his . . .

LENNY & WALTER. (*unison*) . . . leg . . .

LENNY. . . . and his . . .

LENNY & WALTER. (*unison*) . . . jaw . . .

LENNY. . . . and his . . .

LENNY & WALTER. (*unison*) . . . back.

HENRY. How did it happen, Lenny?

LENNY. They spit it out, that he had broken his . . .

LENNY & WALTER. (*unison*) . . . skull.

HENRY. How was he hurt?

LENNY. Oh, they didn't want to talk to me, but they had to after that. They had to tell me that it was inside, that he was bleeding . . .

LENNY & WALTER. (*indicating, and in unison*) . . . here . . .

LENNY. . . . and . . .

LENNY & WALTER. (*unison*) . . . here . . .

LENNY. . . . and . . .

LENNY & WALTER. (*unison*) . . . here.

HENRY. Couldn't you stop it?

LENNY. Can I give him these things?
HENRY. Couldn't you stop it?
LENNY. That he's bleeding in his . . .
LENNY & WALTER. (*unison*) . . . brain.
LENNY. So, all right, these tubes, and these wounds, but could I leave him his things?
HENRY. No? (*WALTER exits.*)
LENNY. How about his cap? How about that, you . . .
HENRY. Lenny.
LENNY. . . . cocksucker. . . !
HENRY. Lenny!
LENNY. . . . shiteater!
HENRY. Son.
LENNY. Tell me how to do it.
HENRY. Is that what you want?
LENNY. Aren't you my doctor?
HENRY. Yes. How do you feel?
LENNY. Not good. How would you feel?
HENRY. Do you want to talk about that?
LENNY. No. He's hurt so bad.
HENRY. I know.
LENNY. You know what they're trying to do? They're trying to take him off the machines.
HENRY. Yes.
LENNY. It seems like they can have their way. I'm trying to fight it, but it seems like they can do anything they want, and what I say doesn't make any difference.
HENRY. Nothing's been decided.
LENNY. Oh, my lawyer doesn't think there's any chance. He says the law's clear . . . and I infer also that it's on their side all the way. I don't like that. I don't like procedures or instructions or supervisors.
HENRY. How about at work?

LENNY. Or there, either.

HENRY. But you have a job.

LENNY. Yeah. Oldsmobile.

HENRY. How long have you been there? (*pause*) How long, Lenny?

LENNY. Quite a while. Four years.

HENRY. You must like it.

LENNY. Ah, well, they have their procedures too, but I get along all right. I know what to expect of them, and they know what to expect of me. I'm set.

HENRY. What do you do?

LENNY. I'm a test driver.

HENRY. Is that right? That sounds very exciting.

LENNY. No, not at all. Not really. It's very routine. But no one looks over my shoulder in particular. They don't tell me what to do, except not to go too fast.

HENRY. Do you?

LENNY. Not anymore. In the beginning I might have. There's one turn where I like to go, but you do it so many times, it's not a challenge.

HENRY. You test every model?

LENNY. No, oh no, every car. Not by myself. I'll drive, maybe, one out of every five. There's four other men in the same kind of work.

HENRY. I didn't know they were so careful.

LENNY. Sure. I'm the last person to touch that car at the plant. It comes off the line, I hop right in, fire it up, go straight through this big double door they have. Then out the door there's a sharp left, then a long, sweeping turn to the right—that's the one I like—up the ramp and into the parking lot where they load them on the trucks. I don't do that, I just park it there and walk away. It's about a hundred yards, but first of all you can hear if there's something wrong, most of the time. You turn that key, you're checking the engine. You check your instruments. You have turns left, and right, so you've got a check there for the steering and the suspension. You hit the brakes at the top of the ramp. It's laid out. You'd be surprised how much we catch.

HENRY. I see. How long have you been a test driver?

LENNY. The whole time. Four years.

HENRY. I didn't know . . . that's what test drivers did.

LENNY. You're not alone in that.

HENRY. What do you mean?

LENNY. I just thought I'd call it that and see how it sounded. Test driver. Lenny Keller, test driver. What they call it is "job description, lot attendant." I park cars. I just have a lot of criteria today, so I changed the definition.

HENRY. Oh, I see.

LENNY. Oh, well, good.

HENRY. So you're not a test driver?

LENNY. I told you, I made that up.

HENRY. Do you do that often?

LENNY. That horse you rode in on, Doc, he's headed south; maybe you could catch him.

HENRY. I'm sorry, Lenny.

LENNY. Forget it.

HENRY. Would you like me to leave?

LENNY. What happened, you feeling insecure now? On top of everything else, I have to look out for everybody's feelings. My lawyer wants to leave. You want to leave. Leave.

HENRY. I don't want to leave.

LENNY. Then stay. Do what you want to do. That's what I'm doing. Everybody else is working for some point or principle or law. I'm working for my boy.

HENRY. I know.

LENNY. I was raised to be more concerned about people than . . . things. And if the law and the courts were more in that direction, it'd be better. I'm not a very well educated man—if I were I wouldn't be parking cars for a living—but I know that much.

HENRY. I'd have to agree with you.

LENNY. It's not that I'm bragging. It's not as though I'm at the top looking down at the world. I'm down there myself. Everything I have achieved I have had to work for and fight for. But I have never lost my concern for people.

HENRY. You should feel good about that.

LENNY. I do. I am never discourteous. And you must never discourage people. That reflects on you. (*pause*) . . . shit . . .

HENRY. What's wrong?

LENNY. Nothing.

HENRY. You sure?

LENNY. I was just starting to feel sorry for myself again.

HENRY. Shouldn't you?

LENNY. No.

HENRY. What did you mean, "again"?

LENNY. I don't want to go into it.

HENRY. All right.

LENNY. I was just feeling sorry for myself, that's all. I was just feeling sorry for myself, goddammit.

HENRY. It's O.K., Lenny.

LENNY. No it's not, it's no good. It doesn't accomplish a thing, it doesn't get me anywhere, it doesn't do anything for the boy. That's all that matters. There's no time for that. In a little while that judge is going to decide whether my son's going to live or die, and here I am thinking about myself. I was taught better than that.

HENRY. Were you?

LENNY. Let me tell you something. You think all this is going to be in the papers?
HENRY. Probably.
LENNY. You think I'm going to get in trouble over it?
HENRY. I don't know.
LENNY. Well, I don't care. I don't care about any of that. Only Tommy. You think it's been easy? He's almost two. You know, his mother left us when he was only three months old. My wife. Sweet, huh? In a situation like that, most guys would have just given up, given it all up. I didn't. A lot of fathers would have put him up for adoption. Not me. I didn't lose my job, I didn't go on welfare, I didn't go running to my folks. I didn't fall apart, I didn't start drinking, I didn't start running around. Probably I wanted to do all of those things, but I didn't. You know what I did? I made . . . I became . . . a homemaker. I made a place for my boy and myself, all by myself. Here's what I did that first week: I found a lady that would come in and take care of him during the day, first off; and then I found a day-care I could bring him to as soon as he was old enough. Then I found a store that would deliver food right to the house, and diapers, and formula, and everything. I talked to the doctor; I found out when I had to bring him in, and what for. I went down to the store and ordered books about how to be a single parent. I did all of that by myself. And the last thing I did that week was go out back and put in a sandbox, and I put up a set of swings—three chairs—and I made a promise; I promised the both of us that when he was old enough we'd be out in the backyard and I'd work in the garden while he played in his sandbox, and then I'd swing him on his swing. And I kept that promise. Even though I'd been . . . *abandoned*.
HENRY. You did it all by yourself?

LENNY. That's right.

HENRY. You had no help?

LENNY. Not a soul. Except those that I paid.

HENRY. You didn't ask your folks?

LENNY. I told you I didn't want to go into that.

HENRY. All right. It sounds like a lot.

LENNY. It was.

BEN. (*entering at the rear of the mainstage*) All right, Keller.

LENNY. Yes, sir.

BEN. (*noticing HENRY*) Oh, hello, Henry. How are you?

HENRY. Counselor, nice to see you.

BEN. You're . . . examining my client?

HENRY. We're just talking.

LENNY. That's right, sir, we were just going over the situation.

BEN. Good, good. It seems the situation has changed somewhat. We may be hearing more from you than I expected.

LENNY. What's happened, sir?

BEN. You're amicus curiae in this matter, is that right?

HENRY. Yes. Why?

BEN. Well, Keller, I owe you an apology. I was mistaken about some aspects of today's hearing. At least, some of what I thought was going to be the case is no longer the case.

LENNY. What are you telling me?

BEN. I just came from a meeting in the judge's chambers, and he informed me in the course of our conversation that he would rule out no line of questioning in this matter, and that he himself would feel free to inquire into every aspect of the situation.

LENNY. I don't see anything different in that.

BEN. The point is he indicated that he would inquire specifically into your motives for filing the appeal.

LENNY. You said he wouldn't do that.

BEN. I know I did, Keller, but I was wrong. I . . . was wrong, that's all.

LENNY. Well, didn't you argue with him? Didn't you tell him that wasn't part of it?

BEN. Yes. I did.

LENNY. What did you say?

BEN. I told him that I believed it was a case of a father looking out for the welfare of his child. That it was an error to read anymore into it than that.

LENNY. He didn't believe you?

BEN. He didn't disbelieve me either, Keller; he just didn't agree that he should restrict his inquiry in that area.

LENNY. Oh, well, good. I'm glad there was no . . . "crisis of confidence."

BEN. What are you suggesting?

LENNY. Nothing. I was just . . .

BEN. Now listen to me, Mr. Keller.

LENNY. I asked you not to call me that.

BEN. My earlier offer is still open, *Mister* Keller. I'm acting in your behalf because the court instructed me to do so, not because you sought out my services, and certainly not because you're paying for them. This gives me no particular leverage or rights, Mister Keller, except that it allows me to remind you that you have no investment in me. As I told you before, you can have me replaced at any time.

LENNY. All right, I understand.

BEN. Do you want me to continue?

LENNY. I'm sorry, sir. I guess I was out of line.

BEN. You guessed right, Mister Keller . . .

LENNY. Please . . .

BEN. I'll do the best I can for you, and that's all I can do. Clear?

LENNY. Yes, sir.

BEN. Good. I'm sorry about this, Henry.

HENRY. Not at all, Ben.

BEN. I know we can count on you for an objective opinion.

HENRY. Of course.

BEN. All right then. Keller, I'll be back. See you in court, Henry.

HENRY. See you there.

(*After a pause for BEN's exit:*)

LENNY. Touchy, eh?

HENRY. Maybe a little.

LENNY. I think he's doing a good job, though. Don't you?

HENRY. I'm sure he is.

LENNY. I wish he wouldn't call me that, though.

HENRY. What?

LENNY. Mister.

HENRY. Don't you like that?

LENNY. It's all for Tommy. I'm sure he's doing everything he can to help.

HENRY. Of course he is, Lenny.

LENNY. I never call Tommy that, I wouldn't do that to my son. My old man used to call me "Mister Keller" for certain, special conversations. I was older than Tom. But if I'd come home from school with a bad report he'd say, "All right, young Mister Keller, it's time we had a talk." There were certain questions and problems he didn't like to deal with.

HENRY. Don't you think all fathers are like that, Lenny?

LENNY. Oh no, not me and Tommy. Until this happened, I was always there for him, whatever problem or question that he had, not that he had too many at his age, but I was always there, until this. I don't even know how this happened. All I ever wanted to do was be a good father, and be able to hold him.

HENRY. Yes.

LENNY. And now all I do is worry. I worry about him over there that maybe he's in pain. What if he's in pain? I'm worried about what this judge is gonna decide, what he's gonna say. I'm so afraid, I know that this is a "Mister Keller" situation. And I'm worried about what happens if he dies. What'll I do? And now I'm worried about what's gonna happen to me if he does. I wasn't even thinking about that before, but with what he says . . . they're gonna ask me . . .

HENRY. I understand.

LENNY. You know what happened.

HENRY. Yes.

LENNY. Now I feel like I need someone to hold *me,* and there isn't anyone.

HENRY. Well . . .

LENNY. No! There isn't anyone! I'm not gonna give in to that now. Not after what's happened.

HENRY. Would you like to tell me about it now?

LENNY. Oh sure, would you promise to *hold me* afterwards?

HENRY. Tell me, Lenny.

LENNY. That's what Tom and I had. We used to hold each other a lot.

(*From the side, in a reprise of the opening scene:*)

WALTER. . . . all this bears on the question of intent . . .

LENNY. Come here, son, let me wipe away that little tear.

WALTER. . . . the nature and availability of the weapons employed . . .

LENNY. Just throw your arms around my neck, I'll carry you.

WALTER. . . . if no weapons were employed, the type of blows struck . . .

LENNY. You didn't know my old man . . .

WALTER. . . . the degree of force . . .

LENNY. . . . he was the original "Mister Keller."

WALTER. . . . the duration of attack. (*He exits.*)

LENNY. He was. When I was a little boy, older than Tommy, six maybe, but young. And I was lying in bed one night, trying to go to sleep, and he was in the room, and I said, "Dad, you know what I want more than anything?" And he said, "What's that, Mister Keller?" And I said, "Dad, I want to get married." And he said, "Why would you want to go and do a thing like that?" And I said, "'Cause then I wouldn't have to sleep alone." He laughed, he thought that was so funny. It wasn't anything dirty, I didn't know anything, I was just six years old. I just was scared of the dark, I didn't want to sleep alone, I wanted someone to hold me 'til I went to sleep. I used to lie there for hours in the darkness, and I could imagine all kinds of creatures out there, and suddenly my teddy was this big old mean bear, and my bunny had these nasty teeth, and I just knew the walls of my bedroom were moving out, letting all these things in, and pretty soon I couldn't control it anymore and I'd start to cry. And I'd keep on 'cause I knew if I cried long enough and loud enough, someone would come and get me. And, sure enough, it always worked. Eventually, my old man, it'd wake him up, and he'd get up out of bed, and he'd stagger down the hall and open the door, and right off the light would make me feel better. And he'd come into the room and say, "All right, Mister Keller, what's the matter here?" And I'd say, "Daddy, I'm scared." And he'd say, "What do you want me to do about it?" And I'd say, "Just hold me." And he'd say, "You just want me to get in there and cry with you." And that used to make me so unhappy, and I'd say, "Don't cry, Daddy. There's nothing to be afraid of. I don't want you to cry, Daddy, please don't you cry." I couldn't stand the idea that he might. So right away I'd stop, and as soon as I did, he'd . . . he'd get up and close the door and go back to bed. That's the way it worked, and it *did* work. I'd stop; and that was the only way he knew to get me to do it.

HENRY. Yes, Lenny.
LENNY. I promised that I would never . . . ever . . . let my son cry that way, that I'd learn how to hold him so he wouldn't.
HENRY. Yes.
LENNY. But my old man was never comfortable with anything like that, physical or . . . tender . . . particularly between men. But with sex he was O.K., he would joke about it. I would ask him questions, you see.

(*WALTER, from the side, in the voice of LENNY's father, sweet and fierce:*)

WALTER. Go ahead, young Mister Keller, shoot!
LENNY. I'd say, "Why do they call it 'necking,' Dad? Where does that come from?"

WALTER. . . . All right, boy, I'll tell you what they like . . .

LENNY. "And how about 'sparking'? Is that 'sparks flying'?"

WALTER. . . . they like it when you fuck 'em real hard . . .

LENNY. "How about 'spooning'? Is that like 'fit together'? I think that's really sweet."

WALTER. . . . it don't matter if you fuck 'em in the twat . . .

LENNY. "What's it like when you have a girlfriend?"

WALTER. . . . it don't matter if you fuck 'em in the asshole . . .

LENNY. "Will she hold you whenever you want her to?"

WALTER. . . . it don't matter if you fuck 'em where they breathe . . .

LENNY. "Is that what it means when they say you're sweet on each other?"

WALTER. . . . jus' fuck 'em hard, make it hurt . . .
LENNY. "Was it like that with you and my mother?"
WALTER. . . . they like it when it hurts . . .
LENNY. Did she hold you when you had to . . .
WALTER. . . . they like it when you make 'em . . .
LENNY. . . . when you had to . . .
LENNY & WALTER. (*unison*) . . . cry . . . (*WALTER exits.*)

LENNY. I'll bet she did! I'll bet she did!
HENRY. Lenny.
LENNY. That night with Tommy, I was thinking about all that. You get in a mood . . . and you want to be held . . . and there's no one there . . . and these thoughts come back. You don't know what to do.
HENRY. And what happened?

LENNY. He was just crying, that's all.
HENRY. Go on.
LENNY. That's all. I was just holding him and talking to him, and thinking about these things, but he couldn't stop crying.
HENRY. Yes.?
LENNY. . . . he just . . . couldn't stop . . . and I was holding him, and that's when . . . it happened . . .
HENRY. What?
LENNY. His . . . his . . . head . . . it . . . broke. . . . I heard it.
HENRY. And then what happened?
LENNY. He screamed.
HENRY. Then what?
LENNY. He went on screaming. I couldn't make him stop.
HENRY. Then what did you do?
LENNY. I hit him. (*Pause. LENNY is crying.*) But I was holding him when I hit him.
HENRY. O.K., Lenny. It's all right.
LENNY. I don't know what happened. I don't know.
HENRY. It's all right.
LENNY. He's gonna be coming back pretty soon.
HENRY. Who?
LENNY. My lawyer. He's gonna take me in there for the judge. It's a Mister Keller situation for sure. I don't know what I'm gonna say to them.
HENRY. You don't have to say anything to them. You can remain silent, you know.
LENNY. I know that, but I can't just let them do it. I've got to try to explain. If they think I'm just fighting them for my own sake, they won't listen to me. And it's not . . . it's not for me.
HENRY. You know, Lenny, that I'm supposed to give

them my opinon about that?

LENNY. I see.

HENRY. You know that.

LENNY. It . . . doesn't matter.

HENRY. But you knew it all along, didn't you?

LENNY. Yes. But you didn't think I was lying about anything?

HENRY. Were you?

LENNY. No! Except the part about being a test driver, and that was just a joke.

HENRY. Was it?

LENNY. Come on! I didn't even have to talk to you. I may be under arrest, but that doesn't mean I have to say a word.

HENRY. You wouldn't have done it just to try to convince me?

LENNY. No, sir.

HENRY. To gain sympathy? To make things easier for yourself?

LENNY. No, sir. This is only for him. I don't even have to be here. I could just walk out. I could make bail. Don't you think I could? I have a home and a job, I'm not a bum. I'm only under arrest for . . .

HENRY. For what?

LENNY. I've just been charged, that's all.

HENRY. Charged with what? Say it, Lenny.

LENNY. Assault. Assault. But there's no reason to leave. There's no reason to go home. There's no one there.

HENRY. If the judge goes against you, Lenny, what happens?

LENNY. If they take my son off that machine now, he may die.

HENRY. And if he does?

LENNY. I can't think about that now.

HENRY. But if that happens, what will they do with you?

LENNY. They'll charge me again.

HENRY. With what, Lenny?

LENNY. With murder. For killing him.

HENRY. Doesn't that matter to you?

LENNY. No.

HENRY. Some people think that it might.

LENNY. I tell you, it doesn't matter to me . . . what happens to me. Let's look at it the other way for a second, all right? Do you know what happens if I win today, and they leave Tommy on that machine, and I'm right, and he lives? You know what'll happen?

HENRY. What?

LENNY. They'll take him away from me. No matter what, they'll take him.

HENRY. Perhaps.

LENNY. Oh no . . . no. My lawyer made that very clear. No matter what, he's gone. I've lost him.

HENRY. I don't know.

LENNY. It's true. I made him tell me. He said maybe, if they thought it was all right, they'd let him come visit me on a weekend once in a while. That's it, once in a while. Every day I used to drive home, and every day I would look forward to it so much because I knew my son was waiting for me. Even before he could speak he'd get over to the door and be waiting for me. And now that he can talk it was wonderful 'cause he'd meet me and he'd say, "Daddy," and he'd try to say a few words about what he was doing, or what toy he had out, or what he wanted me to see: "Come here, Daddy!" And that's no more. No more. That's the worst thing in the world that could happen to me. And it's already happened. You think I care whether I'm in jail or not, or what they charge me with? I don't care at all, not . . . at . . . all.

HENRY. All right, Lenny.

LENNY. You understand, don't you?

HENRY. I think so.

LENNY. Good.

BEN. (*entering at rear*) Keller?

LENNY. Here we are.

BEN. Still at it?

HENRY. No, I think we're done now.

BEN. Well, thank you for your time, Henry. They're about to start; I think we should get ready to go in. Keller, I brought these things for you. I think it'd be a good idea if you'd put them on.

LENNY. Yes, sir.

HENRY. Well, I'll see you there.

BEN. Thanks again, Henry.

HENRY. My pleasure. (*He starts out, then turns back.*) Lenny . . . is there anybody you'd like me to call? Do you have a friend?

LENNY. No.

HENRY. You have quite a lot to do here today, don't you, Lenny?

LENNY. (*softly*) Yes.

HENRY. You should have a friend. (*He exits.*)

BEN. We should go, too.

LENNY. O.K. He's a nice man.

BEN. Yes.

LENNY. It was nice of you to bring me these clothes.

BEN. It's all right. You should put the tie on first.

LENNY. Oh, O.K. I don't dress up too often, and I'm a little nervous. This is a nice jacket. Did you bring it from home?

BEN. No, they have a little wardrobe here for people in custody.

LENNY. Really? It's not yours, then?

BEN. No.

LENNY. Oh. I see.

BEN. You're having a little trouble there.

LENNY. Yes. Maybe you could help me. I can't see.

BEN. All right.

LENNY. I don't put ties on very often, not like you. I'll bet you put one on everyday.

BEN. Yes.

LENNY. I think when they ask those questions you were talking about, the doctor will be on our side.

BEN. I hope so.

LENNY. Well, he said he would.

BEN. Yes. There, you look fine.

LENNY. Thank you, sir. I guess this is it, the big moment? Mr. Hammerstein, they're not going to put handcuffs on me, are they?

BEN. No, Keller, that's not necessary.

LENNY. They did when they brought me in.

BEN. That's routine when they make an arrest. It's not required here; there's a guard who'll go with us, that's all.

LENNY. That's all right then. You're not nervous at all, are you, sir? I mean, I am, but you do it all the time, you must be pretty comfortable.

BEN. Yes, Keller, I am. But it won't be so bad, you'll see. I'll get the guard now.

LENNY. Thank you, sir. (*BEN exits.*) Thank you. I'm just going to have to make myself settle down now. Settle down. It won't look good at all if I'm too nervous, they won't believe a word. I want to stand up straight, I want to look him in the eye when I speak to him, right in the eye, otherwise he'll think I'm trying to hide something.

BEN. (*offstage rear*) Keller?

LENNY. Isn't that right, Ruthie? Isn't it? That day, when I tried to reach you on the phone, I wish I could have looked you right in the eye, to tell you about Tommy, to face up to it. When you were around, you used to make me so proud.

BEN. (*offstage*) Keller?

LENNY. You used to tell me that: "This person . . . or that person . . . he's no general, you don't have to call him 'sir' all the time. People won't respect you if you do that." You told me all right: "Hold your head up! You won't get in trouble, people won't punish you for acting like a man. Hold your head up!" I'm doing it now, Ruthie. I'm in there fighting for my boy. I made some horrible mistakes, but I'm trying to set them straight . . . I just hope I'm right. I hope I win. I hope he lives. I hope I get to share with him all those things a father should. I especially want to tell him about love, about how, in spite of everything, there's so much love in the world, and how wonderful it is to have some love in your life.

(*Speaking from the sidestage, again as LENNY's father:*)

WALTER. . . . Mister Keller, they like it . . .

LENNY. All that beautiful romance in the world. I'll teach him.

WALTER. . . . when you fuck 'em real hard . . .

LENNY. It's so great on a nice spring day, a boy and a girl holding hands and walking together.

WALTER. . . . don' matter if you fuck 'em in the . . .

LENNY. Or the love between a mother and a father whose children have gone, but their love gets maybe a little quiet, but strong and deep.

WALTER. . . . don' matter if you fuck 'em in the . . .

LENNY. Or the quiet kind of love between two friends who don't talk about it, but know it's there.

WALTER. . . . don' matter if you fuck 'em in the . . .

LENNY. Or that special kind of a love that a parent has for a child, that doesn't have any limits . . .

WALTER. . . . ain't that right? . . .

LENNY. . . . and you just hold them, and watch them grow . . .

BEN. (*offstage*) Mister Keller?

LENNY. . . . and love 'em to death.

END OF ACT ONE

ACT TWO

At the opening of Act II, LENNY is again alone on the mainstage while HIRSCH is at the side. Initially LENNY reads from the judge's decision. HIRSCH is delivering his courtroom testimony, but he speaks to the audience.

HENRY. It's fair to say that these proceedings have ranged, of necessity, into a number of areas that are of great importance to our society at large, our legal system, our medical establishment, and to each of us as individuals.

LENNY. (*reading*) "That the court has the power to entertain and adjudicate this proceeding cannot be doubted . . ."

HENRY. Of course the principle legal question is to identify that point where life ends and death begins, and to provide the medical establishment with a guideline for action, or inaction, in support of that definition.

LENNY. (*reading*) "That the court has the obligation to exercise that power in this proceeding is equally apparent, for not to do so would constitute an abdication of our fundamental judicial responsibility to resolve a real and immediate problem with which we have been confronted."

HENRY. Here the question has been raised in the context of a case of child abuse, in itself an issue of enormous significance to our various professions, and to our society.

LENNY. (*reading*) "In the case of Thomas H. Keller, a

minor under the laws of this state, it is the judgment of the court that the prognosis of the hospital committee stands confirmed."

HENRY. Despite the efforts of individuals and agencies on all levels, both private and public, the incidence of such crimes continues to rise.

LENNY. (*reading*) "It is the judgment of the court that the patient is in an irreversible permanent vegetative coma, that the prospects of retaining or recovering brain function are extremely remote."

HENRY. In this instance these two issues have come together in that we have a father who has abused his child to the point of death now suing to prevent the state from withdrawing life-support measures. My function has been to advise the court on the plaintiff's state of mind, and on the sincerity of his suit. I began my study by attempting to analyze Mr. Keller's state of mind at the time he allegedly assaulted his son. Let me read to you from the medical examiner's report.

LENNY. Tom? Tommy? I'm sorry, son.

HENRY. And I quote: (*reading*) "It was not possible to determine the order in which the various aspects of the assault took place, however, a number of factors point to a relatively brief duration."

LENNY. I'm afraid I've let you down.

HENRY. (*reading*) "Among these factors were blood tests conducted at the time of admission, the absence of signs of the healing process having begun, the absence of all but hemorrhage-induced swelling, hematoma, et cetera."

LENNY. That's an unhappy admission for a father.

HENRY. (*reading*) "My official judgement is that the assault took place in a period of less than an hour or two; my guess is that it took place in a matter of minutes. As for the question of intent, all the injuries are consistent with what we call a rage-conditioned attack as opposed to one of a more deliberate or premeditated nature."

LENNY. You'll have to do it all on you own now.

HENRY. (*reading*) "In support of this, I observe that no weapons were employed, that the skeletal and other external injuries were caused by several different types of blows."

LENNY. I'll be with you, and thinking of you . . .

HENRY. (*reading*) "For example, the fracture of the nose, the fracture of the jaw, and several lacerations and abrasions all seem to have been due to punches with the fist."

LENNY. . . . so don't give up . . .

HENRY. (*reading*) "The fractures of the ribs and back were probably due to kicks."

LENNY. . . . don't let go . . .

HENRY. (*reading*) "The fracture of the skull was due to a very powerful crushing motion."

LENNY. . . . don't let them win.

HENRY. (*reading*) "And the fracture of the leg, as well as the dislocations of the hip and arm are probably the result of the victim's having been thrown against a wall."

LENNY. (*reading again*) "It is therefore the decision of the court in this matter that the extraordinary life-sustaining measures now being taken shall forthwith be terminated."

BEN. (*Entering at the rear of the mainstage:*) Keller? (*no response*) Keller?

LENNY. Hello, sir. I was just looking at the decision again. They must have had it . . . all ready to go.

BEN. Yes. Do you have any questions about it?

TOTAL ABANDON

LENNY. No, it's very clear, I understand it. I did want to thank you, though, for everything you've done to help me.

BEN. I'm sorry it didn't work out the way you wanted it to.

LENNY. Well, no, we did the best we could. And you were completely honest with me about what kind of chance I had, right from the start. I had my eyes open.

BEN. I'm glad you feel that way, Keller.

LENNY. I do. I even thought the judge was . . . very fair.

BEN. He's good.

LENNY. Of course I wish he had decided . . . differently, but I thought he was fair.

BEN. Yes.

LENNY. I *was* a little disappointed by the doctor, though.

BEN. Which one?

LENNY. The one who was here, Doctor . . .

BEN. Hirsch?

LENNY. Yes, that's it, Doctor Hirsch. He gave me the impression he was going to be more on my side. I was disappointed with what he said.

BEN. Expert testimony is often like that, Keller, they like to stay in the middle of the road.

LENNY. I didn't like what he said about me. I didn't think that was called for. And I didn't expect it.

BEN. Well, I . . .

LENNY. But that's . . . that's all right. I'm not a sore loser, that's one thing. There's no point going over and over . . . we did our best.

BEN. Yes. (*pause*) Would you like me to get you something to eat? Would you like anything?

LENNY. No, thank you.

BEN. I relayed your request to Doctor Bellmon. He said he'd drop by if he had a chance.

LENNY. Thank you very much.

BEN. Well, as long as we have some time, Keller, and since you may have further . . . business, the court has asked me to get some information from you, if you don't mind.

LENNY. What information?

BEN. I need a little background, that's all.

LENNY. All right. First I'd like to ask *you* a question, if I can.

BEN. Of course.

LENNY. Is it possible to find out when they're going to carry out the judge's order?

BEN. I think they'll do it very soon.

LENNY. I know that, but does that mean right away? Or in half an hour? I'd like to know exactly, if I could. I know it sounds silly, but my . . . thoughts would be with him . . . if I could know while it's happening. It's not a trade, but then I'll be happy to give you any information you want.

BEN. All right, I'll see what I can find out.

LENNY. Did that Dr. Bellmon say when he was coming by?

BEN. He didn't say when, he just said he'd try.

LENNY. I hope he does. (*BEN exits.*) And how about Dr. Hirsch? I'd like . . .

(*Turning around LENNY is surprised to find WALTER just inside the door* US.)

WALTER. Hello?

LENNY. Oh hello, Doctor, how are you? Come in.

WALTER. I understand you wanted to see me, Mr. Keller?

TOTAL ABANDON

LENNY. Lenny. Just call me Lenny.

WALTER. All right, Lenny, what can I do for you?

LENNY. Well . . . I . . Mr. Hammerstein just went to find out if they were ready to take my son off the machine . . .

WALTER. Well?

LENNY. He'll be right back. He just has to make a phone call to find out. He wasn't going to go over there.

WALTER. Yes?

LENNY. Actually, that's why I wanted to talk to you. I gathered from what you said that you had actually been to the hospital.

WALTER. I go there all the time.

LENNY. I mean to see my son. I listened to your testimony very closely, and I thought I heard you say you'd seen him just before the hearing.

WALTER. Yes. I did.

LENNY. Well . . . I wanted to know how he was.

WALTER. I thought I was very precise about that in my testimony, if you listened.

LENNY. Doctor, I'm not angry about anything at all that you said. You were supposed to give your opinion, and that's what you did, and I don't have any quarrel about it, or any hard feelings. I know you probably don't think very highly of me, and that's all right too. I just wanted to ask you, because you used a lot of scientific terms which I didn't understand, how my boy . . . well, I just wanted to ask how he was.

WALTER. You put me in a rather difficult position, Mr. Keller . . .

LENNY. Lenny.

WALTER. . . . Lenny. We're not in the courtroom now, and I have no desire to add to your anxiety or your unhappiness. But regardless of the kind of terminology I use, my description of your son's condition would have to be rather . . . harsh. (*pause*) What do you want to know?

LENNY. Tell me how he looks.

WALTER. Look, clinically speaking, your son is not . . .

LENNY. I don't want to hear that!

WALTER. He is not alive! Can't you understand that?

LENNY. Now listen to me. Here is what I understand. I work in a plant with twenty-five hundred other people—in good times there's two shifts so it's two times that almost—and there's five buildings and forty-some-odd sections of the line, and on a good day, with nobody out sick, there's maybe ten people that know my name. And with them it's, "Hey, Keller, you wanna have a beer . . ." not, "Why don't you come over to our place tonight, Lenny, there's a game on." And I live in that Town Oaks development, and I wish I could say that after dark the lights in the houses up and down the street are like beacons of friendship, but they're not. See, Ruthie had the friends on the block, and when she left there was a kind of general cooling of opinion towards me, and maybe that's right, but I don't know how to explain that, or turn it around, or break through, or anything; all I know is that now we're not on the sidewalks anymore, we're backyard people. I made myself go out this year to the Fourth of July block party, and I put ten dollars in the contribution box, and I opened up a can of beer and I laughed at the skits they put on, and I held this little American flag when we sang songs, and I watched the fireworks go up, and I stood there all by myself. Not one person spoke to me. In all this world there's only one person who wants to watch fireworks with me, or go to a ball game with me, or who'll kiss my forehead to wake me up in the morning, and that's my son. I know what I did to him. There will never be another moment's peace in my life because of what I did. But as long as he's breathing and his heart's beating—even if he needs some help from a machine—and as long as there are people looking after him and caring about him, then he's living; for me, he's living. That's why I went to court and that's why I'm asking you these questions. Tell me how he looks. I just want to know how he looks.

WALTER. Keller . . .

LENNY. Tell me.

WALTER. All right! He looks . . . he looks all right. Actually, if you were just going by appearances, he'd seem reasonably healthy. His breathing is slow, but deep. Of course that's the way the machine is set up to operate. When I saw him, he was still receiving transfusions of whole blood, but there was no puffiness and his color was good. All right, that's how he looked.

LENNY. Was he moving?

WALTER. Ah . . .

LENNY. Please, Doctor, just tell me.

WALTER. Occasionally . . . yes . . . he moves. But you have to understand that that's due only to some residual neural activity. It doesn't mean anything more than that.

LENNY. What does he do?

WALTER. Ah . . . sometimes there's a twitch or a little tremor. Once in a while the hand will start to close and then open. But these are nothing more than a kind of reflex, they don't signify anything.

LENNY. But he's moving.

WALTER. Yes.

LENNY. And he looks all right.

WALTER. Yes.

LENNY. Thank you, Doctor. I have another question, if I may.

WALTER. What is it?

LENNY. I wanted to ask you what will happen when they take him off the machine.

WALTER. Keller . . . I don't know.

LENNY. What do you mean?

WALTER. I mean exactly that. I can tell you the steps the doctors will take, but I can't tell you precisely how your son's body will respond to those steps. It varies from case to case, and there's no way to predict the exact behavior. The doctors will remove the breathing apparatus, they'll halt certain medications. These are the things that fall into the category of extraordinary measures. After that it's just a matter of time.

LENNY. What about his heart machine?

WALTER. There is no heart machine. His heart went into fibrillation—that's a kind of spasm—a number of times on the way to the hospital and during surgery. They used a kind of electrical machine to restore the beat when that happened. Since then it hasn't been necessary. That's no different from the muscular reflexes I described before, by itself it doesn't mean anything.

LENNY. Then what you're saying is that the only major thing is the breathing. If he could keep on breathing on his own he could . . .

WALTER. He's not going to keep on breathing. He's given no signs of being able to do so without the respirator. To some extent we're able to measure such things, and he doesn't seem to be . . . working . . . with the machine at all. As best we can determine, there's no impulse there.

LENNY. But you could be wrong. I've read about people who . . .

TOTAL ABANDON 49

WALTER. You've read about some very rare cases in very special circumstances where predictions of immediate respiratory failure were wrong. Our ability to judge these things has increased considerably in the last couple of years; and even if we were wrong, even if he went on breathing on his own, the persistence of heartbeat and respiration aren't going to change the simple face that he's in a permanent and irreversible coma. He has no sensation; he will never see or hear. He will never *speak*. He will never *think*. Those are the facts.

LENNY. I've heard of people who've come out of comas.

WALTER. That's a different . . . Keller, I'm not going to go any further. I told you that I don't want to be harsh, and I don't feel an obligation to dash any hopes or fantasies that you want to hold onto. You've asked for my opinion and I've given it to you.

LENNY. Thank you.

WALTER. (*pause*) I'm sorry about your son.

LENNY. That's all right. It's all right now.

WALTER. Well, then, I'll be going.

LENNY. (*with great conviction*) He's going to be O.K.

WALTER. Goodbye, Keller. Lenny.

LENNY. Goodbye.

HENRY. I agree with Dr. Bellmon's assessment that this assault was an act of rage rather than part of a pattern of protracted abuse. Therefore, it seemed to me very possible that the father's appeal to the court was a genuine one, stemming from an honest sense of responsibility and remorse.

LENNY. (*reading*) "Should death occur, its proximate cause shall be deemed to be whatever caused the patient to lapse into the coma in the first instance."

HENRY. Of course, the key words here are: genuine . . . responsible . . . honest. Is Leonard Keller these things? Was his bringing of this suit characterized by these qualities, or was it motivated by a desire to avoid the consequences of his act?

LENNY. (*reading*) "The proximate cause . . ."

HENRY. In my brief observation of Mr. Keller prior to this hearing I found him to be, at least on the surface, sincere, rational, aware of his actions, and, at times extremely remorseful. Nonetheless, as a precaution, I decided to go beyond the normal procedures in such a case and consult with one of the people Mr. Keller had mentioned to me in our discussions.

(*WALTER appears as LENNY's father, on the sidestage as before.*)

LENNY. (*reading*) ". . . should death occur . . ."

HENRY. I asked myself why I felt compelled to go to such lengths in this case. Nonetheless . . .

LENNY. (*reading*) ". . . to lapse into coma . . . to lapse into . . ."

LENNY & WALTER. (*unison*) . . . Coma.

HENRY. . . . I spoke to Mr. Keller's father. . . . Mr. Keller? (*pause*) Mr. Keller?

WALTER. Yes. (*LENNY hears the inner voice.*)

HENRY. Mr. Joseph Keller?

WALTER & LENNY. (*whispering in unison*) Yes.

HENRY. Leonard Keller's father?

LENNY & WALTER. (*unison*) Speaking.

HENRY. My name's Dr. Hirsch. I've been interviewing your son in a court action involving your grandson, Thomas.

LENNY & WALTER. (*unison*) What can I do for you?

HENRY. You know that your grandson has been hurt, that he's in the hospital?

LENNY & WALTER. (*As WALTER exits, unison.*) Yes, I know.

HENRY. I'm sorry there isn't time to come talk to you in person, but I'd like to ask you a few questions.

LENNY. I'll be happy to tell you whatever I can.

HENRY. First, tell me how you heard about it, about Tommy, I mean. Was it in the papers?

LENNY. No. Leonard called first.

HENRY. Is that right?

LENNY. Yes.

HENRY. I was under the impression that . . .

LENNY. That we didn't communicate? No. He calls us every couple of months to let us know about his latest plan or escapade.

HENRY. I didn't know that you spoke with him at all.

LENNY. More or less. His calls aren't so much conversations as they are announcements. He called once to tell us he'd been named Organizer of his town's Fourth of July celebration. A story. Over the years I've learned to be very skeptical. He was always trying to impress me—lying to make me proud. Even this time he didn't call to tell us about Tommy's condition; he called to say that he was going into some kind of special litigation, that he was going to establish legal *precedents*. As I said, I've become very skeptical. The last real contact we had with him was about Ruthie.

HENRY. Yes?

LENNY. That she'd left him.

HENRY. Yes?

LENNY. That she'd been forced to . . .

HENRY. Ah . . .

LENNY. . . . that he'd beaten her.

HENRY. He said that?!

LENNY. More. He said she liked it.

HENRY. (*whispers*) What?

LENNY. Where'd he get an idea like that, that women want to be hurt? You think he'd want someone to beat him? You think he'd like it? (*silence*) I did my best. I'm no different from anyone else. I made mistakes but I set as good an example as I knew how; and look how my love was repaid . . .

HENRY. Yes.

LENNY. . . . with evil. Beating his wife . . . court actions . . . legal precedents . . . nothing but lies.

HENRY. Not dreams?

LENNY. Bad dreams then. I hope he has 'em.

HENRY. Don't we all?

LENNY. You think *I* deserve them?

BEN. (*entering quietly at rear*) Keller?

HENRY. Mr. Keller . . .

LENNY. Do *you*?

BEN. Lenny? (*LENNY gradually becomes himself again.*) It's started now. (*Pause. LENNY only nods.*) I've just spoken to the hospital. They're going ahead.

LENNY. Are they?

BEN. With your son, I mean . . . they're going ahead.

LENNY. Yes, I understand.

BEN. Well . . .

LENNY. He never hit me, Mr. Hammerstein. *My* father, he never did.

HENRY. (*speaking from the side, as before*) Based on all of the foregoing . . .

LENNY. Won't you sit down?

HENRY. I conclude that Leonard Keller's appeal to the court is *not* genuine . . .

LENNY. You said we'd have further business.

HENRY. . . . does not stem principally from a concern

for the welfare of his child.

LENNY. You need background.

HENRY. Consciously or otherwise . . .

LENNY. Listen.

HENRY. . . . his principal concern is for the legal and moral consequences of his act. (*HIRSCH exits.*)

LENNY. I went to run away once. I borrowed one of my mother's purses—a big one with a handle on it—to be my suitcase. I packed my things; and my parents were in the living room when I got downstairs—this nine-year-old with his luggage. He wanted to hit me then. But he didn't. He didn't get carried away, he just looked at me and after a while he said: "It's very lonely out there, Mister Keller. Come back when it gets too bad." My mother didn't say anything, she just sat there. She knew this was . . . man-talk. Maybe I didn't deserve his love, but I went back up those stairs and I stayed home and quit feeling sorry for myself.

BEN. Keller . . .

LENNY. And when that Valentine came—you have to laugh at this, Mr. Hammerstein—I thought it was for me. For me! That's when I reminded myself that there was my *son,* I couldn't just give in to those feelings. Feeling sorry doesn't matter to a two-year-old; his old man is the only thing that matters; and you have to be worthy of that kind of love, don't you? Don't you?

BEN. Yes.

LENNY. Well, I was, and I want him back. (*with gathering speed*) He wants his oatmeal and raisins in the morning; I put a sandwich in the refrigerator for his lunch; a regular meal together after work. I want him back.

BEN. Keller . . .

LENNY. After that a half hour's TV, I lay out his clothes; we have a walk, water colors, toys, crayons, balls, games, I want him back.

BEN. No . . .

LENNY. He sings. He sings—and if I put a record on the stereo, he dances. At night I tell him his bedtime story and he holds his bottle with one hand and waves with the other . . . he *conducts* me, Mr. Hammerstein, and I want him back!

BEN. Forget it, Lenny!

LENNY. I had a talk with Dr. Bellmon, he said there was a good chance.

BEN. You're lying!

LENNY. No.

BEN. Yes. And you've got to stop lying, and stop feeling sorry for yourself.

LENNY. Don't say that.

BEN. Mister Keller.

LENNY. I told you not to call me that.

BEN. Mister Keller, do you think we're all fools?

LENNY. Please don't call me that name.

BEN. Isn't that what Dr. Hirsch told the court, that you were lying? (*pause*) Well, I'll tell you something else: forget about your son. You're entering into a period when *your* welfare, and *your* future, and no one else's, rides on how you handle yourself, and what you say, and what I or some other attorney says in your behalf. Now if you go on lying to the court, and lying to a jury, they're gonna know, and they're gonna hang you. Do you want that to happen?

LENNY. Hang me?

BEN. You hear me? You want that to happen?

LENNY. What will they do?

BEN. Oh for God's sake.

(*LENNY is oblivious as WALTER appears at the rear of the mainstage carrying a shopping bag.*)

WALTER. Ben?
BEN. Come in, Walter. Like to try your luck?
(*WALTER sets the bag down unobtrusively.*)
WALTER. Can you step outside for a moment?
BEN. What's the matter?
WALTER. We need to talk.
BEN. All right. Keller, will you think about what I said?
LENNY. Sure.
BEN. Think about it. It's time you woke up to the facts. If you don't start . . .
WALTER. Ben . . .
BEN. All right, Doctor. Excuse us . . . Lenny.

(*They exit. LENNY goes to the bag, is beginning to open it when HIRSCH enters.*)

HENRY. Hello, Lenny.
LENNY. Hello.
HENRY. May I come in? (*pause*) The others were talking outside—I thought you might like someone to keep you company. (*The bag is temporarily forgotten.*)
LENNY. You talked to my father.
HENRY. Yes, I did. I also went to the hospital, Lenny. I saw your son.
LENNY. (*whispered*) Thank you.

HENRY. You must have been very angry.

LENNY. (*abruptly*) I wasn't trying to get out of anything. Why did you say that?

HENRY. I didn't.

LENNY. You said "the legal and moral consequences" of my act.

HENRY. I didn't say you were trying to avoid them. I think it's why you stayed here. Why you didn't make bail.

LENNY. Please leave now.

HENRY. I'm scared of you, Lenny.

LENNY. No.

HENRY. I'm scared. Everybody is. Just like you . . .

LENNY. No.

HENRY. "I used to lie there for hours in the darkness, and pretty soon I couldn't control it anymore and I'd start to cry. And eventually he'd get up, come down the hall, open the door into my room . . . " (*LENNY begins again to open the shopping bag.*)

LENNY. What's the matter here?

HENRY. ". . . and I'd say, 'Daddy, I'm scared. I'm lonely, just . . .'" (*The significance of the contents of the shopping bag begins to register on LENNY. He looks up to HIRSCH.*)

LENNY & HENRY. (*unison*) "'. . . hold me.'?"

HENRY. I know. Why were you so angry? (*LENNY begins to remove something from the bag.*) Don't do that yet, Lenny. It's not time. Tell me why you were so angry.

LENNY. My son loved me.

HENRY. Didn't other people love you? (*LENNY looks inside the bag once more. Now he closes it.*)

LENNY. Not as much.

HENRY. Yes.

LENNY. I told you what happened, I told you. He just couldn't stop.
HENRY. Couldn't stop what, Lenny? Crying?
LENNY. Loving me.

(*BEN and WALTER enter.*)

BEN. Lenny?
HENRY. What is it?
BEN. Your son is gone. (*Pause. HENRY sits.*)
LENNY. What?
BEN. It's over. They just phoned Dr. Bellmon.
LENNY. Is that right?
WALTER. Yes.
LENNY. Did anybody . . . did they check to make sure?
WALTER. I'm sure they did, Lenny.
LENNY. What . . . what will they do with the body?
WALTER. I imagine they'll take it over to the morgue. That's required.
LENNY. At the end there wouldn't have been any pain at all, would there?
WALTER. No, I'm sure there wasn't. You know this was always . . . just a matter of time. It was always in the cards.
LENNY. Yes, I know. I understand.
BEN. Despite what I said before, I want you to know that you have my sympathies. I know that no matter what, this can't be . . .
LENNY. Yes. Thank you.
BEN. Well . . .
LENNY. (*interrupting*) Do you want to talk about punishment now?
BEN. What?

LENNY. Do you want to discuss my punishment?
BEN. (*nonplussed*) Henry?
HENRY. Yes.
BEN. *Dr. Hirsch.* (*Finally HENRY stands.*)
HENRY. All right. (*pause*) How soon do you expect a new charge, Ben?
BEN. I suppose right away. I'm sure they have it ready.
HENRY. Do you know what it is?
BEN. I have a pretty good idea, but I couldn't swear to it.
HENRY. Why don't you find out?
BEN. (*taking the hint*) O.K., yeah, sure. Walter? (*BEN and WALTER start out.*)
LENNY. Doctor Bellmon?
WALTER. Yes.
LENNY. Could I talk to you for a minute?
WALTER. Well . . . (*He looks to HENRY for guidance as BEN exits.*) . . . Henry?
HENRY. What is it, Lenny?
LENNY. You were right about the wall.
WALTER. What do you mean?
LENNY. I threw him against the wall. (*LENNY's tranquility leave WALTER breathless.*)
WALTER. Oh.
LENNY. Do you want me to tell you what happened?
WALTER. Ah . . . I'm not sure . . .
LENNY. If you wanted to tell me what was wrong, I could explain it. For the record.
WALTER. Of course . . . that would be very helpful . . . (*Again he looks to HENRY.*) . . . but maybe this isn't the time to go into it.
HENRY. I think it's quite all right, Walter.
WALTER. Well, if you're sure, I . . . I'd . . .
HENRY. Go ahead.

WALTER. All right, let's see . . . of course his single worst . . . injury . . . was the fracture of the skull . . . if you. . . ?

LENNY. Yes. Yes, I was holding him too tightly, with is head cradled in my arm . . .

WALTER. Where, exactly?

LENNY. Here. I've already mentioned this to Dr. Hirsch. I didn't mean it to happen, but I think I squeezed too hard. I heard a sound.

WALTER. What kind of sound?

LENNY. A cracking.

WALTER. I see. Well . . .

LENNY. (*to HENRY*) Why did you call my father?

HENRY. He says he feels sorry for you, Lenny.

LENNY. No! I told you everything you needed to know.

HENRY. You didn't tell me *what was in it for you.*

LENNY. (*to WALTER*) Where is he? Are you sure he's in the morgue?

WALTER. Y-yes.

LENNY. (*back to HENRY*) See? Didn't I tell you how it is at the factory? Didn't I tell you how it is where I live?

HENRY. You started to tell me about feeling sorry for yourself, but you wouldn't finish.

LENNY. That has nothing to do with it.

HENRY. That has everything to do with it.

LENNY. No!

HENRY. Your father says you're a liar, Lenny. Why don't you prove him wrong?

LENNY. It's very personal. I don't want to talk about it now.

HENRY. Then tell me about your wife. Tell me about Ruthie.

LENNY. That's not part of it, either.

WALTER. Henry . . .

HENRY. You don't want to tell me how you felt about necking with her? How was it, kissing her?

LENNY. I told you, I don't want to discuss it, not with my son just this minute passed away.

HENRY. All right then, let me read to you. There may be something here that will remind you of what happened: (*HENRY begins to read from his notes.*) "And I was lying in bed one night . . ."

LENNY. What I had with Ruthie, the romance that we had, was the most important thing in my life.

HENRY. " . . . And he said, 'Why would you want to go and do a thing like that, *Mister* Keller?'"

LENNY. You didn't even ask me about sparking with her . . . maybe I could tell you something about that.

HENRY. " . . . It wasn't anything dirty . . ."

LENNY. Sparks are like sparks flying, which reminds you of fire, and everything that romance is about when one person has another person.

HENRY. You're not telling me what I want to know, Lenny. *Tell me why!*

WALTER. Stop this, Henry, stop this.

LENNY. Don't you want to hear about it?

WALTER. No, I don't! I can go to my office, and sign my report, and then I can go home and try to forget that I ever heard any of this . . . sickness.

LENNY. Do you think I'm sick?

WALTER. I don't know what I think, Keller. I've seen hundreds of cases of child abuse, and, God help me, all I can ever think is that it's . . . evil . . .

HENRY. Yes.

WALTER. . . . Evil. You told me, and you lawyer, and the court, over and over again, that your only concern was the welfare of your child. Well, he's been officially dead now for all of about ten minutes, and here you stand telling me how you *did it*. I don't want to understand these things.

LENNY. But you do.

WALTER. No.

LENNY. You do these things.

WALTER. I don't! Lots of people *don't!* He doesn't! Ben Hammerstein doesn't! This is enough. Henry . . .

BEN. (*entering at rear*) What's going on here?

HENRY. Look who's here, Lenny. (*to BEN*) Did you get the new charge?

BEN. (*uncertain*) . . . Yes . . .

HENRY. All right, Lenny . . .

WALTER. There's nothing there, Henry. He's empty, can't you see?

HENRY. Is that true, Lenny? Are you empty? (*Brief pause. HENRY goes on softly:*) I don't think you are. Anything but that.

WALTER. It's finished, Henry.

HENRY. Perhaps you're right. Perhaps we should just go now. That charge'll keep, won't it, Ben? (*BEN nods. After a beat:*) You don't mind, do you, Lenny, if we leave? Maybe you'd rather be *alone.* (*pause*) Let's go then. (*HENRY begins to usher the others out.*)

LENNY. Wait. Don't go.

HENRY. Yes, Lenny?

LENNY. Don't leave me.

BEN. What's this all about?

LENNY. (*turning to WALTER*) What's next? I was holding him too tightly, with his head cradled in my arm . . .

BEN. What's this all about?

LENNY. . . . what's next? (*BEN can only shake his head mutely.*) His nose, is that right? And his jaw? That was my fist. Punches. Three or four, I'm not sure. And I think . . . I used . . . yes, it had to be, my right hand.

WALTER. Look, Henry . . .

LENNY. I was still holding him with my left, so it had to be my right that I hit him with.

WALTER. No . . .

LENNY. It's very difficult to swing through in that position.

WALTER. Stop it!

LENNY. After that I dropped him. I dropped him on his back, sort of in a sitting position . . .

HENRY. Tell him, Lenny.

LENNY. And after I had kicked him, and he was over in the center of the room, and he wasn't crying anymore, and I got down on my hands and knees so he could look at me if he wanted to . . .

WALTER. No . . .

LENNY. . . . and then I knew, and then I had to say it, I had to say it again . . .

HENRY. Yes, Lenny?

LENNY. (*to an imaginary infant son*) Come back. Come back over here, son.

HENRY. (*reading again*) " . . . And pretty soon I couldn't control it anymore and I'd start to cry . . ."

LENNY. Honey, come here, honey . . .

HENRY. " . . . And I'd keep on 'cause I knew if I cried long enough . . ."

LENNY. Give me some lovin', baby.

HENRY. ". . . eventually he'd wake up, and he'd come into the room, and he'd say, 'All right, *Mister* Keller . . .'"

LENNY. That's what Dad says.

HENRY. Tell me now, Lenny!

LENNY. He told me everything I know about loving. I was always feeling sorry for myself. I was always wanting people to be sparking and necking with me, but he taught me better.

HENRY. ". . . And I'd say, 'Daddy, I'm scared . . .'"

LENNY. Cut out the necking shit, and give 'em what they want.

HENRY. " . . . Dad, I want to get married . . ."

LENNY. Cut the love shit, and give 'em what they want.

HENRY. " . . . I'm sad, Daddy. Just hold me . . ."

LENNY. Fuck 'em real hard . . . that's what they want!

BEN. Stop it now.

HENRY. ". . . Just hold me, Daddy, please hold me . . ."

LENNY. Fuck 'em 'til it hurts . . . that's what they want!

BEN. Enough, Henry!

HENRY. (*no longer reading*) No, Mister Keller!

LENNY. Fuck 'em 'til they cry . . . that's what they want!

HENRY. No!

LENNY. That's what they want!

HENRY. Mister Keller!

LENNY. That's what they *DESERVE!*

HENRY. (*hissing triumphantly*) Yesss!

LENNY. Damn right! I wish I could have given *her* what she deserved. I shoulda done it when I had the chance. Right here, number one! You think it bothers me if you walk out that door? Not a bit. In fact . . . (*Standing over, and referring to, the imaginary child:*) . . . I'll give you something to remember me by. You think you can leave, but everybody's gonna get what they deserve. That's what my old man taught me, and he made damn sure I got it straight. (*To the child, with cruel force:*) Ain't that right, *Tommy*?

HENRY. Yes.

LENNY. You think you can look up at me with those big ol' eyes, like I was the moon and the stars? Well I ain't. I'm just the mean old sonofabitch that brought you into the world. You might as well get used to it. You can cry as much as you want, and you can love as much as you want, but you're just . . . gonna get . . . what you deserve. Hear?! I don't want your tears. I don't want your love. I want . . .

HENRY. What?

BEN. (*taking a step towards LENNY*) Swine.

LENNY. *I* used to cry like that, just like that. Don't think I don't hear me in you, 'cause I do. But I know better, and I'm gonna show you.

BEN. You swine.

LENNY. Because I want . . .

HENRY. Go on!

LENNY. Because I want . . .

HENRY. What's the charge, Ben?!

LENNY. Because I want . . .

HENRY. The charge. . . !

BEN. MURDER!

LENNY. . . . what *I* DESERVE! No goddamn love — *hurt me back!* No goddamn friend — *hurt me back. . .* !

WALTER. (*fearful*) No . . .

LENNY. I want what I *deserve* . . .

WALTER. (*into the silence*) Christ.

LENNY. (*turning on HENRY*) And you, too! Isn't that right, you son of a bitch? . . . you, too.

HENRY. Yes.

LENNY. (*to BEN*) And you. (*. . . and WALTER . . .*) And you. (*. . . and turning front, after a pause*) Lonely bastards. (*After a pause WALTER exits.*)

HENRY. Will you continue as his attorney?

BEN. Yes.

HENRY. I'll help.

BEN. There's a formal proceeding . . . an arraignment. Can he . . . ?

HENRY. Yes, I think so. You'll come, won't you, Lenny? (*LENNY only nods, rises, begins to put on his tie. BEN takes a step toward LENNY, as if to help with the tie.*)

BEN. Do you need . . .

LENNY. (*softly*) No.

HENRY. It's all right. Thank you, Ben. (*As LENNY finishes with the tie, BEN exits.*) Nice work, Lenny, nice work.

LENNY. Is it O.K.? (*They are facing one another, only a short distance apart.*)

HENRY. Yes, yes it is. (*One takes a step toward the other.*) I did what you wanted, Lenny. (*A pause. HENRY turns away, refers to the bag.*) Would you like to keep these? (*LENNY nods.*) I'll see you in a little while, then. (*pause*) Rest now, Lenny. (*HENRY exits. LENNY picks up the bag, looks into it.*)

LENNY. Look what I brought you. (*He takes from the bag a ball cap with the face of an elephant on the peak, a face cloth covered with birds, a bottle of shampoo. Finally he holds a small pajama top with ponies and coyotes printed on it. Now he gently unfolds it, carefully holds it up to his own chest, as though checking for fit. Quietly, and with pride:*) That's my boy . . .

BLACKOUT

END

Other Publications for Your Interest

PAST TENSE
(LITTLE THEATRE—DRAMA)

By JACK ZEMAN

1 man, 1 woman, 2 optional men—Interior

This compelling new play is about the breakup of a marriage. It is set on the day Emily and Ralphy Michaelson, a prosperous middle-aged couple, break off a union of 27 years. As they confront each other in their packed-up living room one final time, they alternately taunt and caress one another. She has never forgiven him for a petty infidelity of years ago. He has never forgiven her for her inability to express grief over the long-ago accidental death of their youngest child. In a series of flashbacks, Mr. Zeman dredges up the pivotal events of his characters' lives. Barbara Feldon and Laurence Luckinbill starred on Broadway in this at times humorous, and ultimately very moving play by a talented new playwright. "... rich in theatrical devices, sassy talk and promising themes."—N.Y. Times. "There is no doubt that Zeman can write. His backbiting, backlashing dialogue has considerable gusto—it belts out with a most impressively muscular vigor and intellectual vivacity."—N.Y. Post.

SCENES AND REVELATIONS
(ALL GROUPS—DRAMA)

By ELAN GARONZIK

3 men, 4 women—Platform set

Set in 1894 at the height of America's westward movement, the play portrays the lives of four Pennsylvania sisters who decide not to move west, but to England. It opens with the sisters prepared to leave their farm and birthplace forever. Then a series of lyrical flashbacks dramatize the tender and frustrating romances of the women. Rebecca, the youngest, marries and moves west to Nebraska, only to find she is ill-prepared for pioneer life. Millie, a bohemian artist, falls in love with the farm boy next door; when he marries a woman without Millie's worldly aspirations, she is crushed. Charlotte, a nurse, is rejected by her doctor on religious principles. Only Helena, the eldest, has the promise of a bright and bold life in California with Samuel, the farm's manager. However, Rebecca's tragic return east moves the sisters to unite for the promise of a better life in England. "A deeply human play ... a rocket to the moon of imagination," Claudia Cassidy—WFMT, Chicago. "Humanly full ... glimmers with revelation," Elliott—Chicago Sun-Times. "The play is a beauty," Sharp—WWD. "A deep understanding of women and their relationships with men," Barnes—New York Post.

Other Publications for Your Interest

A MAP OF THE WORLD
(ADVANCED GROUPS—DRAMA)
By DAVID HARE

7 men, 4 women, plus extras—2 Interiors

This new play by the author of *Plenty* "is an ambitious work which brings together in heated discussion a young left wing journalist and a right wing expatriate Indian novelist. The settings are a Bombay hotel where they are attending a world poverty conference and the British film studio where the Indian author's experiences are being turned into a film. Throughout the play, life and fiction overlap . . . One of the issues is the sexual jealousy that arises over the men's competition for the favours of a promiscuous American actress staying at the hotel. Also on the agenda: idealism vs. cynicism; the West's arrogance in its handling of Third World problems; the alleged evils of Zionism; and the journalist's fervent belief in the necessity for change."—London Sunday Express. "It is a pleasure to hear a stage echoing to such issues and such talk."—London Standard. "A rich and complex play built around a series of antitheses: the Third World and the West, fiction and reality, irony and committment, reason and passion, the personal and the political. Yet for me what makes it the most mature and moving of Hare's works to date is its gut conviction that once we lose our Utopian dreams we have lost everything."—London Guardian. (#15620)

NANAWATAI
(ADVANCED GROUPS—DRAMA)
By WILLIAM MASTROSIMONE

10 men, 1 woman, plus chorus of female extras—Unit set

The intrepid Mr. Mastrosimone, heretofore the author of studies of character such as *The Woolgatherer*, *A Tantalizing*, *Shivaree* and *Extremities*, has here set his sights on an epic scale. Shortly after the Soviet Union invaded Afghanistan, Mr. Mastrosimone managed to get himself smuggled into that beleaguered country via Pakistan. There he spent several weeks with the Afghani rebels, observing their often futile attempts to resist the Russian blitzkrieg. All of the resistance he witnessed was not futile, though; he also observed the capture and execution of a Soviet tank crew. It was this incident which inspired *Nanawatai* (an Afghani word which means "sanctuary"). The story is told through the dual points of view of a Russian tank crew member and an Afghani rebel, as a chorus of village women impresses upon us the effect on the citizenry of all the bloodshed (not unlike, of course, in a Greek tragedy). "Hard-hitting and probing . . . alive with issues and conflicts of both a political and personal nature."—Hollywood Reporter. "It has the ritual power of Greek tragedy."—L.A. Times. (#15975)

Other Publications for Your Interest

LAKEBOAT
(ADVANCED GROUPS—COMEDY)
By DAVID MAMET

8 men—Unit set

This fascinating series of vignettes, staged to great acclaim by the Milwaukee Repertory Theatre, is set aboard a Great Lakes steamer, bound from Gary to Duluth. It focuses in on the eight-member crew, the hardhats of the steel waterways, all but one of whom are "lifers." The other character is a young college man who has been hired to replace the night cook. He is the closest thing to the central figure. ". . . the show has much of Mamet's poetry of the inarticulate, the ritual, tribal double-talk that makes sense underneath the ludicrous patters of our lives."—Chicago Tribune. ". . . a banquet of meaty acting parts."—Milwaukee Sentinel. (#14017)

GLENGARRY GLEN ROSS
(ADVANCED GROUPS—COMIC DRAMA)
By DAVID MAMET

7 men—2 Interiors

Winner of the London theatre equivalent of our Tony Award, this scalding comedy went on to take Broadway by storm, winning the Pulitzer Prize for drama in 1984. Never has Mr. Mamet's ear for the rhythms of actual, contemporary speech been more keen than in this tale of cutthroat real estate salesmen competing against each other for the money of unwary customers. One suavely vicious salesman, Richard Roma, is in the lead for the monthly sales award: a new Cadillac. Another, Shelly "The Machine" Levene, a former top salesman, is now riding a streak of bad luck on a smile and a shoeshine, hoping to turn his luck around. All are dependent upon an office manager named Williamson to give them the vital "leads" to new customers. Williamson, meanwhile, is pitting them against each other to drive up sales. In the first act, composed of three scenes, we meet the salesmen, vying for position as they gulp their cocktails in the local Chinese restaurant. The second act becomes a sort of "who done it" as the scene shifts to the office, where a burglary has taken place. The vital leads have been filched the night before, possibly by one of the salesmen. In the end, Williamson screws Roma out of his car and nabs the bag man. "Crackling tension . . . ferocious comedy and drama. A top American playwright in bristling form."—N.Y. Times. "Wonderfully funny . . . a play to see, remember and cherish."—N.Y. Post. "Mamet is . . . a pure writer, and the synthesis he appears to be making, with echoes from voices as diverse as Beckett, Pinter and Hemingway, is unique and exciting."—Newsweek. (#9058)